Warren Buffett

The Ultimate Guide to Accumulate Wealth And Invest Like Warren Buffett

by Frank Hunter

© 2016 Frank Hunter
All Rights Reserved

Table of Contents

Table of Contents

Introduction

Chapter 1 – Why Warren's Worth Your Interest

Chapter 2 – Key Qualities That Made The Self-Made Rich Successful

Chapter 3 – The Mega-Wealthy Mogul's #1 Most Potent Trait

Chapter 4 – In The War Room With Warren Buffett

Conclusion

Disclaimer

While all attempts have been made to verify the information provided in this book, the author does not assume any responsibility for errors, omissions, or contrary interpretations of the subject matter contained within. The information provided in this book is for educational and entertainment purposes only. The reader is responsible for his or her own actions and the author does not accept any responsibilities for any liabilities or damages, real or perceived, resulting from the use of this information.

Introduction

Today, Warren Buffett is worth an estimated sixty billion dollars.

And that's a very general estimate. In reality, he's worth at least a couple billion dollars more than that. But what's a margin of a few billion dollars when you're already in the black by *at least* sixty billion?

Tomorrow, the exact number attached to Buffett's net worth will be bigger than it is today. By the time you get your hands on this book, it will be bigger still. It's very possible that the general estimate of Warren's fortune has surpassed seventy billion by the time that you're reading this.

You might be thinking: *Yeah that's a lot of money, he's rich, I get it. What's your point?*

My point is that—just like the carefully planned investments that grew his billion-dollar empire—Warren's ongoing financial success is a sure bet. People always say the rich get richer. Well, Warren Buffett exemplifies that nugget of conventional wisdom to an absurd degree.

So how does he do it? And more importantly, how *did* he do it? How does any man get to where Warren is now, earning upwards of fifty million dollars in a single year? How did a boy born into poverty grow up to become one of the wealthiest people to ever live?

This book will teach you how Warren Buffett does it, how and *why* he got there, and—most importantly—how *you* can follow his example to amass extraordinary wealth of your own.

Chapter 1 – Why Warren's Worth Your Interest

What makes Warren Buffett a billionaire of particular interest? What makes him an industry titan worth emulating over, say, Bill Gates? Or Henry Ford?

In a moment, we'll discuss what Warren Buffett has in common with these and other mega-rich moguls. But first, let's talk about what makes him unique among the financially successful.

Warren Buffett, by his own admission, isn't a trailblazer. When asked at a seminar how he personally defines innovation, Buffett humbly responded, "Well, I don't *do* a lot of innovating in what I do."

Wait a second: a billionaire who *didn't* get there by innovating? But that completely contradicts the "common sense" beliefs most people have about getting rich!

After all, don't insanely wealthy people get rich off their *ideas*?

Don't you need that groundbreaking billion-dollar *idea* in order to bank like Warren Buffett?

Apparently not.

You see, unlike Henry Ford or Bill Gates—both of whom *innovated* entirely new industries into existence—Buffett merely stepped into the market, learned all he could about a handful of businesses, and proceeded to amass his incredible wealth by intelligently *allocating his resources*. He made his fortune not as an inventor, but as an *investor*.

This bodes very well for the rest of us. While few people will ever be graced with a stroke-of-genius idea that makes them the next Mark Zuckerberg or Elon Musk, we're *all* investors.

We *all* have the capacity to make better choices with our money. We *all* can learn how to intelligently allocate our resources so that one dollar earned and invested becomes two, or three, or even thousands.

But What If I'm Not An Investor?

But I'm no investor, some people reading this will balk. *I've never made an investment in my life!*

Actually, you are and you have whether you like it or not. You wouldn't have been able to purchase this book otherwise.

You've invested your time into whatever it is you do to earn your living, and you've agreed to be compensated for your time in currency.

Really quick, read the previous sentence again.

Now look at it again, but this time I want you to disregard all but the first five words of the sentence, and the last. The core meaning stays exactly the same:

> You've invested your time into ~~whatever it is you do to make money, and you've agreed to be compensated in~~ currency.

Yes, currency itself—the naked cash sitting in your wallet, purse, or savings account right now—*is an asset you're invested in!*

But few people naturally think about money in these terms. To the average person without any financial background, money is a vague, intangible green-paper substance.

Of course, this is ridiculous. Money is a "good" that serves a function, and it's no more abstract than any other asset. Money has supply. It has demand. It has a definite value that fluctuates from day to day.

The currency you own is an investment with variables like any other. It just so happens that as far as investments go, currency is a relatively poor one.

"Cash is always a bad investment," Warren once explained during an interview. "All you know is that the dollar is going to be worth less ten, twenty years from now...that's true of almost any currency that I can think of."

Warren often likens cash to oxygen. You need enough oxygen around you to breathe, and you need enough cash around you to be secure. But a surplus amount of oxygen isn't necessary, and—as long as you know how to make wise investments—the same can be said for cash. Hence, Buffett has always advised that people exchange their surplus cash for more "productive" assets.

What makes an asset "productive?" Well, we'll get into the brass tacks of Warren's advice in great detail later. The main point here is that—whether you like it or not—you're *always* an investor. So you might as well be a good one. And while you're at it, why not become a *great* one?

And make no mistake, anybody can learn how to be a *great* investor. A great investor is someone who puts their money to work for them. Great investors can become wealthy people very quickly.

Not only that but—as you'll learn in the next chapter—the advantages that come with knowing how to make good investments extend far beyond the realm of finance.

Chapter Recap:
- Warren Buffett built a fortune by carefully allocating his resources. You can do the same to help achieve any level of wealth that you aspire towards.

- We're all investors whether we like it or not—with the asset that is currency being our default investment. You can benefit greatly by exchanging your currency for more productive assets.

Chapter 2 – Key Qualities That Made The Self-Made Rich Successful

In the previous chapter, we established why investment—Warren's particular vehicle to wealth—is an avenue to riches that's accessible to everybody.

But now, let's take a moment to paint in broader strokes. You need more than good investment chops to be successful. You also need to adopt certain character traits and qualities.

You see, the self-made rich all have different ways in which they came into their wealth. Some, like Bill Gates, "innovated" entirely new industries into existence. Some, like Warren Buffett, simply invested money into other people's profit-bearing businesses to share in their success. Others, even simpler still, merely set out to provide a needed good or service and ended up doing it so well that they made fortunes.

But for all the endless variables that make every financially successful individual unique, there are a few universal traits that all of them—Buffett included—share with one another on some level.

Quality #1 - The Self-Made Rich Are Fascinated and Fulfilled By What They Do

Just imagine the following:

Bill Gates is a fairly average teenager living in the early 70's.

He wakes up late, drags himself out of bed, and at once he's overwhelmed by an all too familiar force of mounting dread. He absolutely loathes the day he has ahead of him.

After a full hour of restless procrastination, the young Gates finally ambles his way into the garage and flicks on the light.

There—crouched in the corner like some monolithic gargoyle—sits the extremely costly, extremely *unwanted* "present" Billy's father has forced on him: a top of the line, cutting-edge computer.

Looking towards the machine, Gates massages his temple and lets out a sigh.

"Well…better get back to studying this boring hunk of junk," he groans. "After all, these stupid computer things are going to make me the richest man on Earth one day."

End scene.

Now, tell me, does that sound like a likely scenario to you?

Or do you think Gates' attitude towards computers was probably *exactly the opposite?*

Do you find it much more likely that Gate's jumped out of bed every morning thrilled to get back to work on his latest software project? That he fascinated himself with his computer all throughout the day? That he pecked away at his keyboard well into the wee hours of the morning? That he nearly had to be pried away from the thing with a titanium re-enforced crowbar?

We know for a fact which of these two portraits is correct. We know for a fact that Microsoft only began as a young man's burning passion for computers. It was out of that passion that a billion-dollar business eventually bloomed.

Warren Buffett's story is no different.

"I get to do what I like to do every single day of the year...I tap dance to work every day," Warren once explained. "...You ought to be happy where you are working. I always worry about people who say, you know, 'I'm gonna do this for ten years, I really don't like it very well, but I'll do ten more years'...that's a little like saving up sex for your old age...not a very good idea."

Even as a boy, Warren was fascinated with numbers and statistics and how they all fit into the bigger picture. He invested in bulk-packaged "commodities" like chewing gum and Coca-Cola only to resell them individually around his neighborhood at a profit.

He strategized his newspaper deliveries so effectively that he was given charge over the most lucrative routes in the area. A professional career in finance suited him like a glove.

Time and time again, the stories of the self-made rich exemplify this basic principle: do what you love, or at least something you *like*. Even if that thing isn't something classically profitable like software development or finance, you'll be better off doing it. You'll be more likely to find ways to monetize your passion because its' something that you genuinely enjoy you doing.

Quality #2 - The Self-Made Rich Invest In Themselves With Brutal Honesty

As a young man Warren realized that he lacked the fundamental ability to communicate with other people effectively. To correct the weakness, he enrolled in the Dale Carnegie course for effective communication. To this day, Buffett acknowledges Carnegie's teachings as an important contribution to his long-term success.

But Warren never recommends the course to others directly. When he relates his experience with the Dale Carnegie program, it's the concept of overall self-betterment that he means to endorse: the concept of *investing in yourself*.

"Invest in as much of yourself as you can," Buffet stated more plainly on a different occasion, "you are your own biggest asset by far."

Most people have some notion of this concept. But as you'll soon learn, any *good* investment requires a careful examination of the assets in question. And when it comes to examining *ourselves*, it's all too easy for our egos to get in the way.

Introspection is not immediately rewarding—few people willingly choose to occupy their time with the act of thinking in itself. Even fewer people choose to engage in the act of thinking for the sole purpose of pondering their own flaws and failures.

Warren has said, "I insist on a lot of time being spent, almost every day, to just sit and think. That is very uncommon in American business. I read and think. So I do more reading and thinking, and make less impulse decisions than most people in business. I do it because I like kind of life."

If you truly want "the kind of life" that most people dream of having, you too must spend a lot of time in thought. You must examine why you aren't where you want to be in life with brutal honesty. Only by identifying your weaknesses can you then begin to invest in the necessary solutions.

Quality #3 - The Self Made Rich Are Grateful…And Being Grateful Leads To Greater Opportunities

The human mind, I'm convinced, is able to exist in one of two basic modes of operation:

1. The Mode of Victimhood
2. The Mode of Gratitude

At the core, this concept boils down to the difference between having a "negative" outlook on life and a having a "positive" outlook on life. But there's some important nuance going on here that that bears consideration.

Think about someone you know in your life that isn't successful in the slightest. Would you describe that person as somebody who's even remotely "grateful?"

Or—more likely—are they something more akin to "whiny?" Do they always have an excuse for why they aren't where they want to be in life? Is nothing ever their fault? Is the world—in their eyes—always, somehow, *against them?*

Now consider all the mental energy that a person like this constantly exhausts to rationalize where their own shortcomings. Making excuses to keep a delusional worldview intact is endless, tireless work for the mind. Over time it molds that person's mode of thinking into something ever-critical.

Soon, the persistent victim develops a keen eye for all things negative. At the same time, their capacity to focus on the positive weakens from neglect until it ceases to exist.

And once that happens, their failure as a human being is almost certainly set in stone.

"Chains of habit are too light to be felt until they're too heavy to be broken," Warren famously stated in a rare moment of departure from his typical upbeat demeanor.

Entire books have been written on this key quality alone. Good habits are the bedrock of success. The most important habit that a person ever forms is the habit of their thinking: their *mindset.*

Grateful thoughts are a habit that gives way to a positive mindset. By training your brain to hone in on the good things that happen to you rather than the bad, you train your attention to focus to on the positive.

And when you develop a keen eye for the positive, you become infinitely more likely to recognize good opportunities when they come knocking on your door.

Good opportunities are—of course—extremely valuable. But only when they're seized with due enthusiasm.

Before you move on to the next chapter, I want you to take some time to really think about the things you should be grateful for. Warren Buffett's words of wisdom to an American youth foundation audience may offer you a good place to start:

"I was born in 1930, and at that time one out of fifty births in the world were in the United States. So I came in against fifty to one odds. I would have been a disaster if I had been born in Afghanistan or Peru.

I won the lottery the day I was born by being born in this country. So have you. You were five times more likely to have been born in China...or India...or some other place where it would not have been as easy to exploit the full potential of your talents. So we've all won the lottery in that respect."

Set this book aside and take some time to identify and appreciate the good luck you have been granted. Go ahead and do this now.

...Welcome back. Now. There's still one major trait we've yet to discuss that is—without a doubt—the "special ingredient" successful people use to fly high into the stratosphere of financial achievement. It's the metaphorical rocket fuel for wealth, and it's also the subject of our next chapter. Can you guess what it is?

Chapter Recap:

- You won't be successful doing something you hate…even if the thing you hate is a "safer" choice for making money. Do something you enjoy.

- Identify your weaknesses and invest in the solutions. This will make your most important asset—yourself—all the more valuable.

- Choose to live your life in the "Mode of Gratitude," rather than the "Mode of Victimhood." Being grateful for what you have tunes your perception towards new opportunities.

Chapter 3 – The Mega-Wealthy Mogul's #1 Most Potent Trait

One more hint for the subject of this chapter: what is Warren Buffet's most famous moniker? He is known as the '*What*' of Omaha?

That clue should reveal the one trait in particular which stands above the rest when it comes to making people wealthy beyond belief.

Have you made your guesses?

Warren's most famous moniker is, of course, "The *Oracle* of Omaha." The trait, in a word, is *foresight*.

Being able to accurately predict the future is the most profitable ability in existence. When you can foresee where the market's headed, you can be the only one who capitalizes on an incoming trend.

Foresight also allows a person to examine a scenario and prepare for any bumps in the road that could arise on down the line. Foresight allows you to avoid tragedy and mitigate disaster.

The rest of this book is tethered to the running theme of foresight. That's because investment—and wealth accumulation in general—is tethered to it as well.

So how does one cultivate foresight?

"Behavior becomes a habit," says Warren. Like any other character trait, foresight is a behavior you can implant into your life until it forms into a second-nature habit.

Going forward, you must always make it a priority to ask yourself, "How will this decision effect my future?" as often as you can. In all things, think of the end result and how it meshes with your goals.

For example, one major area where many people suffer from a lack of foresight is with the problem of accumulating debt.

"As a general matter—as a one piece of specific financial advice—I would say avoid credit cards...just forget about 'em." Warren told an audience of young people at the Nebraska Educational Forum.

"The American public loves credit cards. But if you start revolving debt on credit cards you're going to be paying eighteen or twenty percent. You can't make progress in your financial life going around borrowing money at eighteen or twenty percent..."

It's worth noting, perhaps, that Warren's investment company has great financial stakes in the business of credit cards. The fact that he tells a group of young people to actively avoid a product in which he's invested ought to reveal something about his character.

A more pragmatic man in Warren's position might toe the line by telling the impressionable audience that debt is a useful tool that should be handled wisely. Warren Buffett, however, makes sure his true thoughts on debt are known outright.

His words are the naked truth. Debt *should* be avoided in all forms and at all costs. And have no delusions—debt can almost always be avoided.

Debt can always be avoided, you say? What about college debt? Isn't that an exception where the cause is a worthy one?

College debt is a great example. Right now, a generation of young people are bemoaning the burden of their student loan debt. But ask yourself, was hundreds of thousands of dollars' worth of debt really necessary to achieve their diploma?

All around the United States are smaller, less extravagant, and much less *expensive* community colleges. Many states' financial aid programs fully cover the cost of their tuition. Nearly all of these colleges are designed to transition a student's credits to more prestigious universities.

So when I hear a young person complain about college debt, the first question on my mind is, "Well, did you take out loans for *four* years of extremely expensive university when you could have done two of those at a more reasonably priced community college instead? And missed out on nothing but the full 'college' experience?"

Of course, hindsight is 20/20 and nobody hasn't made mistakes born of youthful naivety. If you're knee deep in college debt, or if you have debt of any form, don't be discouraged. Think about it as an opportunity to reinforce why the habit of looking ahead is so important. That's a very valuable lesson, and it's worth paying the toll to absorb.

...But doesn't this principle of foresight contradict the "positive mindset" quality described in the previous chapter?

Despite always advising other people to live in the mode of gratitude, Warren still recommends keeping one eye open for potential road bumps in the future. "I've got partner that says: all I want to know is where I'm going to die so that I never go there," Warren once said.

Don't be a Doubting Thomas, but don't be delusional skewed towards the positive in your perspective either. In all things, life's about maintaining a proper balance.

Chapter Recap:
- Foresight is the most lucrative quality one can have.

- Push yourself to ask "How will this affect me in the future?" for all of your decisions.

- Always keep an eye out for potential weak spots in your plans.

Chapter 4 – In The War Room With Warren Buffett

Time to get down to brass tacks. We've laid down the groundwork for your financial success by learning all about the key qualities of a financially successful person. Now let's get into the nitty-gritty of amassing wealth with some of Warren Buffett's most profound investment advice.

The simplicity of these four financial maxims will surprise you.

Warren's Wealth Tactics #1: Invest In <u>Productive</u> Assets, They're More Valuable Than Gold

How does Warren Buffett feel about gold—perhaps the world's most well-advertised investment opportunity?

"If you took all the gold in the world it would roughly make a cube sixty-seven feet on a side…it would be worth at today's market prices about seven trillion dollars. That's probably about a third of the value of all the stocks in the United States.

 So you can have a choice of owning a third of all the stocks in the United States or you can have a choice of owning that little block of gold which can't do anything but kind of shine there and make you feel like Midas or Croesus or something of the sort…"

"…For seven trillion dollars: there are roughly a billion acres of farmland in the United States. They're valued at about two and a half trillion dollars…you could have all the farmland in the United States, you could have about seven Exon Mobiles, and you could have a trillion dollars of walking around money…"

"…I f you offered me the choice of looking at some sixty-seven-foot cube of gold—looking at it all day, touching it, fondling it occasionally, and saying 'do something for me' and it says 'I don't do anything, I just stand here and look pretty'—and the alternative to that was having all the farmland in the country, everything: cotton, corn, soybeans; seven Exon Mobiles; and a trillion dollars of walking around money…call me crazy, but I'll take the farmland and the Exon Mobiles.

Warren's logic stands on its own. Scarcity-based investments will never expand your wealth in the way that profit-garnering investments have the potential to do. When it comes to investing: go business or go home.

Warren's Wealth Tactics #2: Know Exactly What You Need To Know Because It's <u>All</u> You Need To Know

This might come as surprise: Bill Gates is a lifelong friend of Warren Buffett and yet, to this day, Gates has never been able to convince Buffett to invest in computers.

That's not because Warren Buffett is a close-minded luddite. Warren Buffett simply prefers to stick to things that he knows. He doesn't understand the market for computers, so instead he continues to allocate his resources into businesses of which he's well informed.

"You might have an entirely different field of expertise of than I would have," Warren has said. "Probably much more up to date in terms of businesses that we're seeing evolve. And you can get very rich if you just understand a *few* of them and understand their future."

Warren's Wealth Tactics #3: There Are No "Balls" When It Comes To Investing To Your Money

Ignore the potential double entendre in that heading. The "balls" I'm referring to are the balls within the context of baseball. For those unfamiliar with the sport, sometimes a player up to bat will find it strategically advantageous to *not* swing at a pitch. This is known as a "ball", but there are only so many balls allowed before the batter is considered defeated.

There is no such case when it comes to investing. The only way you can "strike out" with investing is by taking swings at opportunities that aren't any good.

"...I can wait there and look at thousands of companies' day after day, and only when I see something I understand—and when I like the price at which it's selling—*then* I swing..."

"...[Investing] is an incredibly advantageous game, and it's a mistake to think that you have to have an opinion on everything...

"...You only have to have an opinion on a few things. In fact, I've told students if when they got out of school they got a punch card with twenty punches on it and that's all the investment decisions they got to make in their entire life...they would get *very* rich, because they would think very hard about each one. And you don't need twenty right decisions to get very rich. Four or five will probably do it over time."

Warren's Wealth Tactics #4: Invest In Businesses with Management You Trust

Here's where Warren's well-earned status in the world of business really serves him. With the connections that he's made over the years, he has the opportunity get to know the people running entire industries on a very personal level, and he goes through great lengths to do just that (with a fine line drawn at certain point for legality and ethics' sake, of course).

By doing so, Warren gives himself an incredible advantage in the world of investment.

The rest of us, of course, do not have such direct access to the movers and shakers of the corporate world. Luckily, we do have access to some very effective surrogates.

Even before he was a well-connected mogul, this tactic was one of the major lynchpins for Buffett's investment success.

He read interviews, public statements, and seminar transcripts done by the CEOs of the companies he was researching.

He formed well-grounded opinions on their character and analyzed their potential as leaders. After all, he was—in a sense—putting his financial wellbeing into these peoples' hands by investing in their businesses.

In this regard, you can and should do the same for any business in which you are inclined to invest. You may just find that their newly instated CEO is a well-connected kook who's already run several corporations into the ground.

Chapter Recap

- Invest in productive assets that earn a profit, rather than investing in things with scarcity-based value and praying that they continue to remain unobtainable.

- Stick to investing in businesses you know well within markets that you fully understand. While it's important to diversify, narrowing the amount of different assets you invest in will allow you to understand all of them more thoroughly.

    You absolutely need to research your opportunities, and you only have so much spare time to research each different business.

- If you aren't certain about an investment, don't do it. Wait for an opportunity to come along—or go seek one out yourself—that you understand well and feel very sure about it.

- A good leader can make or break a business. Make sure you do your research on the management of company before you put a fraction of your financial wellbeing into that person's hands.

Conclusion

True wealth is made when your money works for you. A well-grounded investment strategy can be anyone's vehicle to wealth—and it can even get you there in a relatively short period of time.

True, it may take years to master the ins and outs of investment on the level that Warren Buffett operates, but now that you've read this you book you've forged a golden compass for yourself: pointing you in all the right directions.

Return to this book often throughout your journey, memorize its principles, and do more research as required to fill in the gaps for your own investment strategy.

Your fortune is literally waiting for you out there in the world. Only you can take the steps necessary to reach out and take it. Any form of achievement requires action. You know you want to achieve great riches, so what will your next action be?

Lessons Learned

Traits For Success In General:

- Enjoy whatever it is you do to make your living. Even if it's a less-than-lucrative profession, wealth can absolutely be achieved through responsible saving and good investment strategies either way.

  You're likely to have more money to invest if you like what you do on a day-to-day basis. Do not structure your life so that you work a job you hate for one big "pay off" at the end.

- Be brutally honest with yourself in order to come to terms with your current weaknesses. Unless they are acknowledged, your current weaknesses eventually become your permanent weaknesses. Bear witness to your faults so that you may overcome them.

- Invest profusely in yourself. Maximize your talents and minimize your weaknesses.

- Live life with a grateful outlook. Train yourself to see positive events as they happen and you will also become more likely to recognize valuable opportunities when they arise.

- Make it a priority to practice foresight. Always have an eye on the horizon for potential snags in your progress. Learn to recognize the trends and patterns all around you.

Tactics For Accumulating Wealth:

- Excess currency is always a poor investment. Put your surplus cash to work by investing it into productive assets.

- Avoid debt at all costs. Avoid credit cards in general. If you can't afford it now, you shouldn't buy it. You'll enjoy any purchase infinitely more when it comes without an interest markup.

- Scarcity-based investments such as those in precious metals are a poor choice compared to a well-researched investment in a prospering business.

- Look at the investments you're interested in from every angle. Limit your financial field of vision to fewer prospects so that you can devote more attention to each of them and therefore understand them more completely.

- Approach every investment opportunity as if it were the only investment you could make in your entire lifetime. Pretend like the money you plan to invest is irreplaceable, and ask yourself if you would still make the investment.

- A company's management is just as—if not even more—important than their product, service, or branding. Pay attention to the people that run the businesses you're investing in. Research their replacements as they arise to make sure that their leadership records are up to your standards.